GOD SAYS, "YOU'RE OK!"

Text by
MARY PAOLINI

Photographs by
HANK MORGAN

Foreword by Louis M. Savary

THE REGINA PRESS • New York

1979
THE REGINA PRESS
7 Midland Avenue
Hicksville, New York 11801

© 1979 by The Regina Press

Library of Congress Catalog Card Number : 79-63245
ISBN : 0-88271-032-X

FOREWORD

The essential theme of this book is God's unconditional loving acceptance of children. In GOD SAYS "YOU'RE OK!" the texts portray many situations children face in life, positive ones as well as others where we grownups might be critical, impatient, or angry at them — the very situations where God would prefer that we say, "You're OK" to them.

Saying "You're OK" may mean "I love you," or "I forgive you," or "I accept you just as you are," and "You are worthwhile." It does not necessarily mean "I approve."

Learning to like themselves is, for children, a first step in learning to love others and to be loved by them.

Louis M. Savary

When I can figure out how to do something by myself,
God says to me, "You're OK."

God, I'll bet You know
I'm learning more each day.

Well, yesterday I made a thing.
You know, a thing.
It's not a big thing
but I made it all by myself.
I didn't ask anybody for help.
But I felt so good when I finished it
that I showed what I had made to my friend.

And Jesus said, "If you believe in me, you can
do the things that I do, too, and even greater
things than these." (John 14:12)

When I like to be alone and quiet,
God says to me, "You're OK."

I am glad, God,
that I don't have to be busy
every minute of the day.

Sometimes
I like quiet time
when nobody's around
so I can see what's in the sand
or look up at the sky
or close my eyes
and pretend I'm on a ship at sea
or flying over faraway lands.

And Jesus said, "Come away by yourselves a
while to a quiet resting place." (Mark 6:31)

When I need someone to listen to me,
God says to me, "You're OK."

God, I'm glad
that I can talk to You
and that You listen to me.
It doesn't matter if I'm sad or glad
or mad about something that happened to me.

You are my friend
and friends know
it's all right for me to feel
just the way I do.

And Jesus said, "Father, I thank you for listening
to me, I know that you always hear me."
(John 11:41-42)

When I am thirsty,
God says to me, "You're OK."

When my friend and I
run and play,
we get thirsty.

God, when You're thirsty
does anyone ever give You
something to drink?
And don't You feel better?
We feel better.

And Jesus said, "If anyone is thirsty, come to
me and drink." (John 7:37)

When I turn to God during sickness,
God says to me, "You're OK."

God, the other day
I was sick and cried because my stomach hurt,
and I had to take medicine to help me feel better.
I asked You
to help me get well soon.

I'm glad that You care for me
even when I'm sick.

And Jesus said, "Your faith has made you well;
go in peace." (Luke 8:48)

When I remember that others get tired,
God says to me, "You're OK."

Because my brother is little,
he gets tired
when we play for a long time.

That's when I say,
"Come on, you're tired.
Let's sit down a while.
Later, we'll play some more."
My brother is my friend, too.

And Jesus said, "Come to me, all of you who
are tired, and I will give you rest." (Matthew 11:28)

When I am full of joy,
God says to me, "You're OK."

Sliding boards are fun.
I like climbing higher and higher
toward the sky,
and when I slide down to the bottom,
I laugh when I feel the air
rush past me.

There are so many things
for me to do
and so many ways to have fun.

And Jesus said, "I have shared this with you,
so that you may share my joy, too." (John 15:11)

When I feel scared and turn to God,
God says to me, "You're OK."

When I'm afraid of barking dogs
or loud noises
or thunderstorms or the dark
or sometimes
of people I don't know,
I can always go
to my mother or my father
or to You, God.
Why?
Because I know
all of you will take care of me
and then I'll feel safe.

And Jesus said, "Take heart, it is I. Have no fear." (Mark 6:50)

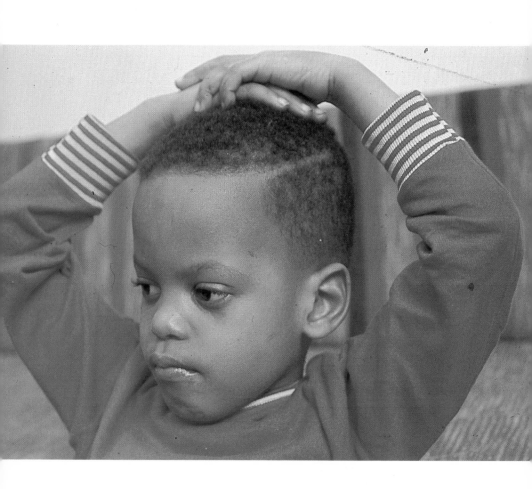

When I go through sad feelings,
God says to me, "You're OK."

I don't know why sad feelings come along,
but they do.
Sometimes they keep me
from having a good time
or make it hard for others
to get along with me.

But I know, God, that You will help me
feel better
so that I'll be happy soon.

And Jesus said, "For the moment you have
sad feelings, but I shall see you again, and then
you will be joyful." (John 16:22)

When I hurt because others make fun of me,
God says to me, "You're OK."

Sometimes other people make fun of me
as if it doesn't matter
how I feel
or that I don't like it.

I am glad I can talk to You, God,
because You understand
how I feel.
I really wish other people
would try to understand
and not make fun of me anymore.

And Jesus said, "Show love to your enemies,
be kind to those who hate you. Treat others the
way you would like them to treat you."
(Luke 6:27, 31)

When I am full of happiness,
God says to me, "You're OK."

I like being happy
because I feel big inside
just like a balloon
that gets bigger and bigger.

I like telling other people
nice things, too,
so they will feel just like I do —
full of glad feelings.

And Jesus said, "I told you how much the
Father loves you, so that you may be at peace."
(John 16:33)

When I accept myself as I am,
God says to me, "You're OK."

I believe, God, that You know
the me deep down inside —
the me that whistles happy tunes
or tries to smile when I really feel sad
or the me that is lonely
when nobody's around.
I know You care for me
just the way I am.

And Jesus said, "My Father will love you, and
both of us will come to you and make our home
with you." (John 14:23)

When I share ice cream with others,
God says to me, "You're OK."

Everybody likes treats,
don't You, God?
Like ice cream in the middle of the day.

I gave my friend an ice cream-on-the-stick
because I had two of them.
And when the ice cream melted on our fingers,
we licked our fingers, too.

And Jesus said, "My nourishment comes from
doing what my Father wants me to do."
(John 4:34)

When I let others go first or have their way,
God says to me, "You're OK."

I like to race to the house
with my friends
to see which one of us
can get there first.
I always want it to be me
but sometimes I let
someone who is littler
get there first.

God, You know it's important
to be first sometimes.

And Jesus said, "Those who want to be first
must start at the last place, showing care to
everyone." (Mark 9:35)

When I work hard to do something well,
God says to me, "You're OK."

I painted a picture
in school.
At first, I didn't know
what to paint
but I tried anyway.

And guess what?
I chose the colors all by myself
and my painting turned out
all right.
My teacher liked the colors
I used, too.

And Jesus said, "These works I do show you
that the Father has sent me." (John 5:36)

When I try to be brave,
God says to me, "You're OK."

Sometimes when I have to do
something hard
or go somewhere new,
I try to be brave and strong
even if I feel butterflies
flying all around inside my stomach.

I'm glad, God,
that I can ask You to help me be —
You know that big word — courageous.

And Jesus said, "There is no need for you to
be afraid, for I give you peace of heart as a gift."
(John 14:27)

34

When I try to find different ways to do things,
God says to me, "You're OK."

Today, God,
I learned a new way
to climb on the bars.
Now that I know
there's more than one way
maybe there are three, or even four ways.

I'll bet if I try
I can find
even more new ways
to do the very same thing.

And Jesus said, "Anything is possible to those
who believe." (Mark 9:23)

When I go someplace new and feel all alone,
God says to me, "You're OK."

This is a brand new neighborhood
and I don't like being here.
I feel all alone
because I don't know anybody.

God, do You think anybody
besides You
understands how I feel right now?

And Jesus said, "I will not abandon you. I will
come to you and be with you." (John 14:18)

When I am happy to see my friend,
God says to me, "You're OK."

One of my friends surprised me
by coming over for a visit.
As soon as I saw my friend
I felt good and happy.

I waved my hand and started to smile.
I could hardly wait
till my friend reached me.

And Jesus said, "I have come that you may
have life, and have it more abundantly."
(John 10:10)

When I visit people who are sick,
God says to me, "You're OK."

When I heard
my friend was sick,
I went to visit him.
I wanted to cheer him up
and make him feel better.

Today I stayed with him
only a little while.
Tomorrow I'll stay longer
and I'll take him a special surprise.

And Jesus said, "I was sick and you visited me.
Welcome into life that will never end."
(Matthew 25:36, 46)

When I take time to help others,
God says to me, "You're OK."

Why do zippers get stuck
and kite strings break
and wheels fall off toys?

When something breaks,
it's hard to fix it all alone.
So when my friend has something
that needs fixing
I go over and help.
It takes time to help but that's OK.
He's my friend.

And Jesus said, "Your care for others is the
measure of your greatness." (Luke 9:48)

When I ask questions to help me understand,
God says to me, "You're OK."

I am glad that I can ask
my mother and my father
all kinds of questions
like "Why are fire engines red?"
or "Where do rainbows come from?"
or "Where do puppies go when they die?"

Sometimes they don't know
answers to my questions.
But many times they can tell me
about things I really want to know.

And Jesus said, "When the Spirit of truth comes,
he will guide you into all the truth." (John 16:13)

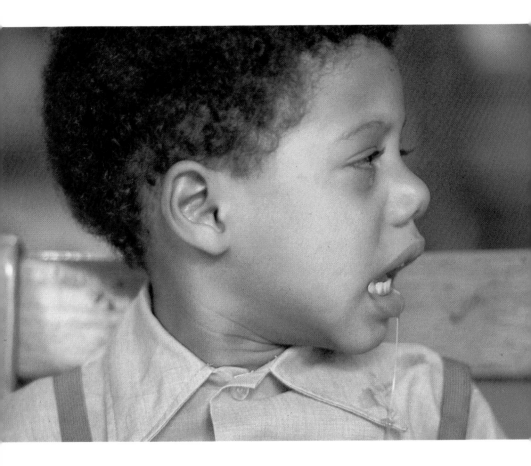

When I care for others,
God says to me, "You're OK."

My friend cried today
and I didn't know why.
So I put my arms
around my friend
and said, "I'm sorry
that you're so sad."

My friend cried for a little while
and then stopped.

And Jesus said, "Blessed are those who weep,
for they shall be comforted." (Matthew 5:4)

When I greet my friends,
God says to me, "You're OK."

"Hello" is such a happy word, God.
I like when my friends say "hello" to me.
And it's nice to say "hello" back
and watch them smile.
It doesn't matter
who says "hello" first, does it?

God, You say "hello" to me every day
in many ways,
don't You?

And Jesus said, "You should act toward each
other, as I have acted toward you." (John 13:15)

50

When I help others learn something new,
God says to me, "You're OK."

God, do You know one way
I can show people I care for them?

I can help them learn —
a new game
or how to make something new.
I like to share
what I know,
especially when others don't know
what I know.

And Jesus said, "Go and teach others all that
I have taught you." (Matthew 28:19-20)

When I enjoy being together with friends,
God says to me, "You're OK."

When I am with my friends,
I feel happy and bubbly.

Sometimes
we sit together and tell stories
and laugh and giggle.
We like to play tag, too,
and chase after one another.

Can You tell, God,
how much I like my friends?

And Jesus said, "Everybody will know you
are my friends because you love one another."
(John 13:35)

When I care for someone,
God says to me, "You're OK."

Deep down inside, God,
I have good feelings
when I do something that shows
I care for others, too.

How can You tell I care?
Well, sometimes
I share peanut butter and jelly sandwiches
with my friends,
or my toys,
or almost anything I have.

And Jesus said, "Love one another in the same
way that I love you." (John 13:34)

When I place trust in my friends,
God says to me, "You're OK."

Do You know, God, when I feel great?
When I trust my friend
to take care of me,
especially when I say, "I'm scared
because I don't know how to do that."

I like to be with others
who show me something new
and take care of me
both at the same time.

And Jesus said, "Don't be afraid. You trust God,
now also trust me." (John 14:1)

When I ask others to be my friend,
God says to me, "You're OK."

Today in school
a new boy joined our class.
He seemed shy,
so I talked to him.
I asked him where he came from
and what he liked to do
and what games he liked to play.

We got to know
and like each other.
You know, God,
I think I have a new friend.

And Jesus said, "I call you friends, for I have
told you everything my Father has told me."
(John 15:15)

When I enjoy clowns and magic,
God says to me, "You're OK."

God, have You ever seen
a clown really close up?
I have.
When I went to the circus,
a funny looking clown
came over and asked me to help.

I saw his magic world
and things
I've never seen before.

And Jesus said, "If you know how to share
good things with your children, how much more
will your heavenly Father share good things
with you, if you ask Him." (Matthew 7:11)

When I enjoy the different seasons of the year,
God says to me, "You're OK."

God, I like every season of the year.
Why?
Because in winter I can play in snow
and in summer at the beach
where I can dig and dig forever in the sand
or build a castle — any kind I want,
alone or with a friend.
And in fall and spring
I can listen to the wind.

And Jesus said, "Father, the glory which you
gave me I have given my friends." (John 17:22)

When I enjoy little things,
God says to me, "You're OK."

God, do You know that October
is my favorite month?
Can You hear the noise I make
when my shoes crunch the leaves?
Listen!

And look how high
up in the air
I can throw pine cones.
Watch me
when I let go of a feather.
See how it floats to the ground.

And Jesus said, "Ask and you will receive,
that your joy may be full." (John 16:24)

When I see how beautiful the world is,
God says to me, "You're OK."

God, do You know that the sky
isn't the same color every day?
Sometimes it's blue or white
or even gray.

Some days the sky is full of birds
or clouds that look like soapsuds.

Do You see all those things
from where You are?

And Jesus said, "Blessed are your eyes, for
they see." (Matthew 13:16)

When I like to run and play at the beach,
God says to me, "You're OK."

When I am at the beach,
I can go to the water's edge
and splash water on my face
to cool me off
or run along the shore
or wiggle my toes in the sand
or fill my bucket with water
and pour it over me.
Sometimes
I pour water over my friend instead.

And Jesus said, "The water that I give you will
become a spring bubbling up into eternal life."
(John 4:14)

This page is for your favorite photograph or picture.

Would you like to write to God on this page? You would? Then go ahead. This space is just for you.